Where is Venezuela? Alvaro (Nacho) Palacios , Leonardo (Leo) Nieves

1st edition. February 2018

Printed by Createspace

©Alvaro Ignacio Palacios Arias

©Leonardo Roseliano Nieves Sillié

©Meollo Comics C.A
Phone: (+58) 212-4902556
Email: info@meollocriollo.com
www.meollocriollo.com

Translated by: Daniel Bastidas
Text Correction: Natalia Rasquin.
Design and Illustrations: Leo Nieves
Color: Leo Nieves, Daniel Bastidas, Giuliano Buffi.
Cover Design: Leo Nieves
Backgrounds: Giuliano Buffi

Where is Venezuela?

At Papapa's cozy house
there is an old family deal:
that on every Sunday noon
all come gather for a meal.

Right after the barbecue
Alesia tinkered with her tablet
and received a sudden call
from a far side of the planet.

It was her cousin Jose
who was calling to show
how outside his house
it had just started to snow.

But despite him being so cold
he saw no sweaters, no umbrella,
so, he asked with muddled tone:
Where is Venezuela?

And Papapa very excited
loudly shout an invitation:
"Let us all go on a trip
through a country of exception!"

We are located in the middle
of the Americas' Mainland
right here in the Caribbean
where summer forever stands.

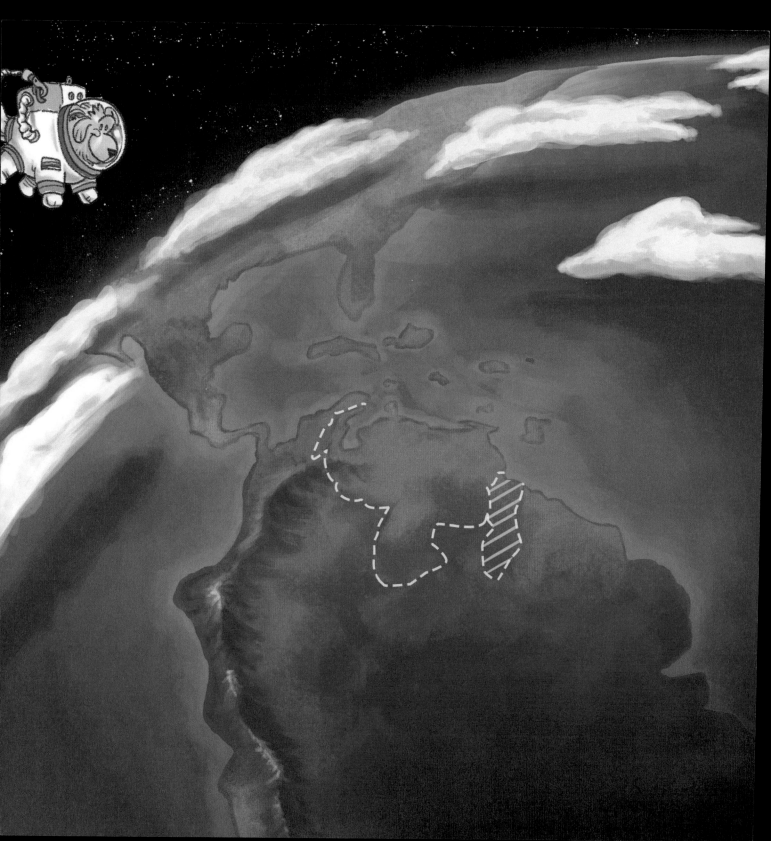

We have a lot of beaches,
unparallel to any other
famous all around the world
for their crystal-clear water.

We also have the "Médanos",
tons of sand kissed by the sun;
rolling down its golden dunes
is for sure the greatest fun!

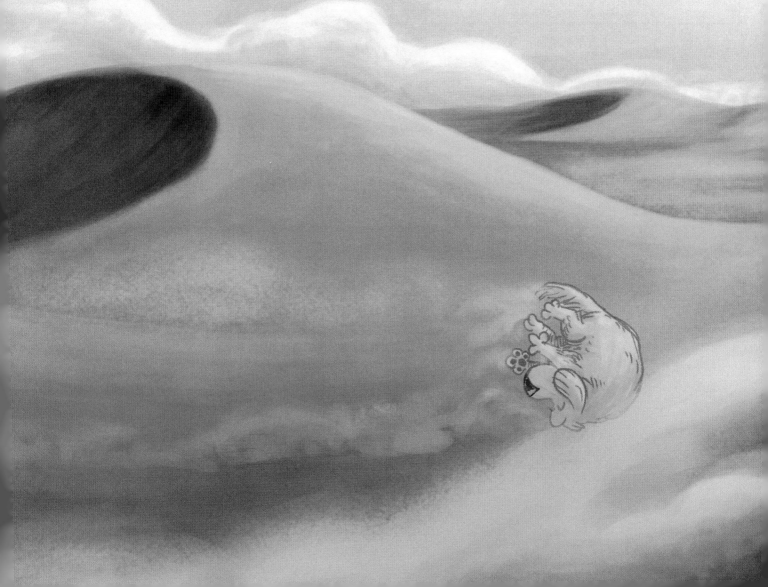

We also have the "Llanos"
named like that for one reason:
It's a vast and green savannah
with a straight line of vision.

We have a tropical rainforest
crossed by rivers deep and might,
with "tepuis" and the Angel Falls;
in the world there's none as high!

We have tall, imposing mountains
crowned with awe-inspiring peaks,
and among its "frailejones"
you can wander just for kicks.

We have quite a super lake
big in size and oh, so smashing!
that God loves to light it up
with a constant flash of lightning.

We also have a magic valley
that surrounds a lively city,
with a mountain that stands out
what a luxury it is, really!

But it's more than just a country
plenty on amazing sights;
Venezuela is so unique
for its people's soul and spice!

People who feel very proud
of their soil and flag alike,
and the country lives within us
being inside or outside.

The answer to the question
was already at reach of hands:
Venezuela will be always
where a Venezuelan stands!

So the family with joy
started dreaming all together
being united in a future
that will shine until forever.

And while such a day arrives
They'll remember from the start:
Where is Venezuela?
IT IS DEEP WITHIN OUR HEARTS!

Dedicated to those who carry Venezuela in their hearts.

Nacho Palacios

He was born in Caracas, Venezuela, in 1976, and likes to create.
His name is Álvaro Ignacio, but everyone knows him as Nacho.
He studied Mass Comunications at the Universidad Católica Andrés Bello
(Andres Bello Catholic University).
He's the creative director and screenwriter for film, radio, television and
Meollo Criollo. He married Carla and since then all his writings are for her.
He loves art, especially pictures made by his daughters, Alesia and Clarisa.
He is filled with excitement, because his son Feliciano Ignacio was recently
born.

Leo Nieves

He was born in Caracas, Venezuela, in 1974, but was raised in Carora, and likes
to paint. His name is Leonardo Roseliano, but everyone calls him Leo.
He studied Illustration at the Instituto de Diseño de Caracas (Caracas Design
Institute).
He's the art director and illustrator for television, advertising and Meollo Criollo.
He married Sylvia and since then all his drawings are for her.
He's a film and soccer fan, especially of the goals scored by his sons,
José Leonardo and Andrés Enrique.

Identify the Regions

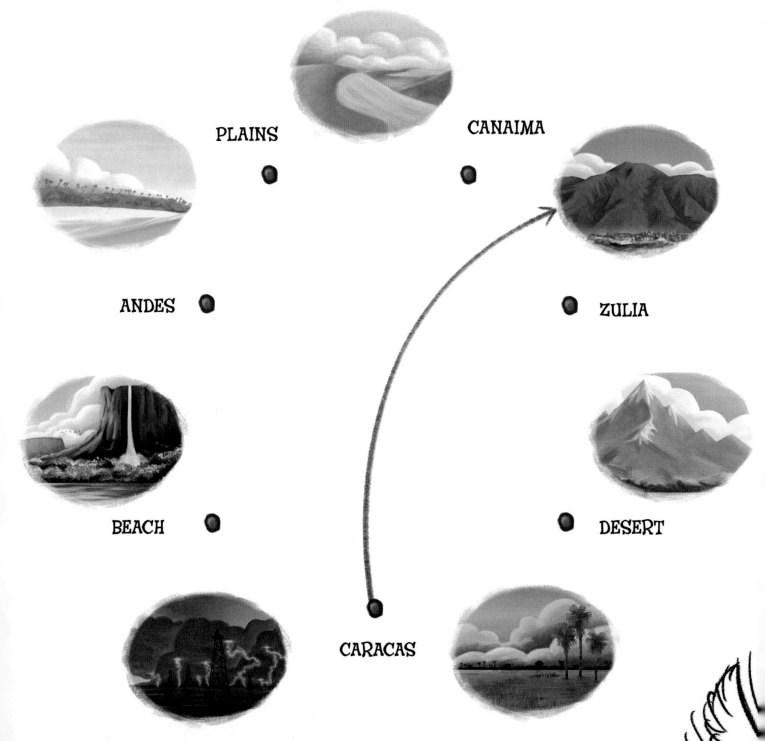

PLAINS

CANAIMA

ANDES

ZULIA

BEACH

DESERT

CARACAS

Color your map

Made in the USA
Las Vegas, NV
06 October 2023

78688419R00024